GUNS FOR
THE HOME GUARD

An attractive volume on the
principal arms issued to
the Home Guard; their use
explained in non-technical
language

BY

K. M. LAZARUS

(Major late Machine Gun Corps)

*Deputy Platoon Commander F Company
No. 1 Battn. Sussex Home Guard*

—

The Naval & Military Press Ltd

Published by

The Naval & Military Press Ltd

Unit 5 Riverside, Brambleside
Bellbrook Industrial Estate
Uckfield, East Sussex
TN22 1QQ England

Tel: +44 (0)1825 749494

www.naval-military-press.com
www.nmarchive.com

THE VICKERS MACHINE GUN

There is probably no weapon light enough to be moved by hand, comparable to the Vickers Machine Gun, in the production of rapid bursts of fire which can be accurately controlled by one man as to direction, elevation and intensity of fire. The gun presents a very small target when in action, and can be tuned up to fire at a rate of approximately 500 rounds per minute, although under normal circumstances, rapid fire does not exceed half this rate. The usual speed is about 125 rounds per minute.

The gun in action weighs about 40 lbs.

By reason of its fixed mounting on the tripod, fire direction can be maintained when a target becomes invisible through fog, gas, darkness, or smoke screen.

The mounting also allows of an all-round traverse, and, if the personnel be sufficiently well trained, of overhead and indirect fire.

There are inherent disadvantages in the gun, such as mechanical breakdowns, steam from the water when it boils, and a very marked flash, but these are overcome by proper attention to the points before and during action.

A normal course of instruction is too lengthy for the average Home Guard unit, but there is no reason why teams should not be trained efficiently to get the gun into action and keep it firing. When once the elementary principles are understood, the vital necessity is for continued practice and constant handling of the gun.

After quite a short time the good gunner works automatically and as well by night as by day.

During the early days of training the gun will probably seem to be just " another thing to be learned," but as progress is made, so will the fascination of the gun grow. Realisation of the amazing simplicity of the action, combined with its almost unbelievable accuracy, soon produce the " mental excitement " arising from a production of rapid and controlled fire, and lead to a real affection for the gun.

Ambition to be the best gunner in the best team is contagious, and competition to handle the gun and tripod a little more efficiently than anybody else, leads to the rapid acquisition of a high standard of efficiency throughout the team.

DESCRIPTION

The gun can most easily be described as a fixed casing (consisting of two parts, barrel and breech casing), containing a series of recoiling parts and also an ammunition feed.

The front portion of the fixed casing is the barrel casing or cylinder through which the barrel passes. This cylinder takes about 7½ pints of water used for cooling the barrel. The water boils after about 500 rapid fire, or about 2,000 rounds at normal rate.

There is an attachment to which is fitted a condenser, thus preventing any tell-tale escape of steam. The barrel casing also carries on its outside the blade foresight and vulcanite screws in the two holes required for the filling and emptying of the water, and, inside, the steam tube with a sliding valve to ensure the proper escape of the steam to the condenser.

The rear part of the fixed casing is the breech casing.

The most important fittings are :—

> On the left, the fusee spring and box, and also the left slide.

> On the right, the check lever and the right slide carrying the collar on which the crank handle revolves.

> On the top, the Tangent sight (graduated up to 2,800 yards) on the outside, and the trigger bar on the inside.

> On the bottom, the sliding shutter.

At the back, the rear crosspiece with the thumbpiece for firing, the safety catch and the traversing handles.

The recoiling parts consist of :—

Barrel, with muzzle cap attachment.
Side plates, which join the barrel to the crank.
Lock (containing the firing apparatus).
Extractor. This is attached to the lock, and its functions are to withdraw the ammunition from the belt and place it in the chamber, and to withdraw the empty round from the chamber for ejection.
Crank, with handle and fusee attachment.

They are attached to the ammunition feed or feedblock by a stud and recess.

They are attached to the fixed casing through the fusee spring, of which the front end is fastened by means of the fusee spring box to the left side of the breech casing, and the rear end by the fusee.

The feedblock is the means by which—by the operation of a slide actuated from the movement of the recoiling parts—the belt is passed from right to left through the fixed casing, and by which each round is in turn placed in position, so that the extractor, gripping the base of the cartridge, can withdraw it from the belt and place it in the chamber.

The gun is fired from a tripod mounting.

The legs of the tripod are attached to a socket into which is fitted the crosshead, which in turn carries the elevating gear.

Each of the legs has its jamming handle. The rear leg is actually left permanently adjusted to suit the No. 1 of the team, and is not altered unless the gun is to be fired from uneven ground. The two front legs, however, are closed each time that the gun is dismounted. When the tripod is set up, care must be taken to ensure that the jamming handles are thoroughly tight, and that they do not work loose during firing. The legs must be adjusted so that the socket is upright. The crosshead is controlled by a clamping screw at the rear of the socket. This screw controls the traverse, and it should always be kept " sticky," so that a slanting tap on the gun handles will not swing the gun too far over.

The gun is attached to the tripod by two pins which pass through fittings on the crosshead —one over the socket and the other at the top of the elevating screw.

Elevation is obtained by adjustment of the elevating screw. This is turned in a clockwise direction to depress the gun and anti-clockwise to elevate.

Practice will enable the gunner to turn the wheel automatically so that each variation is even, and control the strength of his taps in order that an even traverse is obtained.

The ammunition is fed to the gun from belts containing 250 rounds, the belt passing through the feedblock from right to left. The belts are filled either by hand, or by the belt filling machine. Gunners are expected to be able to fill a belt in about twelve and a half minutes by hand, while the speed with which they can work the machines depends largely on their ability to keep the ammunition supply going, and on the state of the pockets of the belt itself.

When belts have to be filled in the field, hand filling is the method normally employed.

Each third pocket in the belt has a long brass tag to mark how far the nose of the bullet should protrude through the belt.

When filled, each belt is placed in a box. Eight boxes should be available for each gun. The ammunition must be inspected periodically, and care must be taken to see that the rounds do not become stuck in the belts, as is inclined to happen if they are left for a considerable time.

MECHANISM

The gun is water-cooled and operated by two agencies.

The explosion of the charge, assisted by the gas striking against the cup at the end of the barrel, drives the recoiling parts of the rear. Later they are carried forward by the action of the fusee spring.

As the gases follow the bullet out of the barrel, they strike the cone and rebound on to the cup screwed on to the front end of the barrel itself, thereby assisting the force of the recoil. As the working parts move to the rear, the fusee spring (which is attached at its front end to the breech casing, and at its rear to the recoiling crank) is extended, and the feedblock is caused to engage behind the next round in the belt. At the same time, the extractor withdraws the round which it has gripped from the belt. As it comes to the rear, the tail of the crank handle is forced on to the collar attached to the breech casing, which causes the crank to rotate. During this rotation, the lock and extractor are drawn further to the rear, while the fusee spring, taking command over the force of the gases and recoil, carries the remainder of the working parts forward.

When the lock and extractor are fully back,

the extractor drops and places the round opposite the chamber.

These parts then join in the general forward movement, during which the round is placed into the chamber, and the feedblock places the next round in the position ready for the extractor. As the forward movement is completed, the extractor is forced up to its original position and grips the round which has been placed in readiness by the feedblock.

The firing pin hole is now ready opposite the firing pin; when the trigger is pressed the gun will be fired and the process repeated.

The firing mechanism itself is contained inside the lock.

WHEN THE LOCK IS DRIVEN TO THE REAR the side lever head (which joins the lock to the connecting rod and crank) is raised, and so causes the tumbler inside the lock to rotate.

Owing to this rotation, the firing pin is withdrawn and the lock spring (which lies between a projection on the forward end of the firing pin and the trigger) is compressed.

Owing to the compression of the lock spring, the nose of the trigger is forced behind the bent of the tumbler as soon as the tumbler is sufficiently rotated. (But as this rotation is continued the trigger does not actually become engaged).

Owing to this continued rotation, the firing pin is drawn further back until the bent is engaged by the bent of the sear, which is forced in position by the sear spring.

WHEN THE LOCK MOVES FORWARD the side lever head presses down on the sear, thus releasing the firing pin, which goes forward until the nose of the trigger engages in the bent of the tumbler and so prevents its further progress.

WHEN THE SAFETY CATCH IS RAISED AND THE THUMBPIECE PRESSED, the trigger bar (inside the rear cover) and the tail of the trigger (which is engaged in the forward end of the trigger bar) are drawn to the rear. The nose of the trigger is thus disengaged from the tumbler, which allows the firing pin to fly forward under the influence of the lockspring.

As long as pressure on the thumbpiece is maintained the gun will continue to fire, as the tail of the trigger will be drawn back each time the lock goes forward, and the firing pin will therefore be carried forward when released from the bent of the sear.

When pressure on the thumbpiece is released, the nose of the trigger will engage in the tumbler and the firing pin will be held back.

CARE OF THE GUN

The more care and attention that can be given to the gun, the more it can be relied upon to function without stoppage in action.

For the daily cleaning, no stripping is necessary. The outside of the gun, and all working parts that can be reached, must be wiped over with an oily rag. The barrel is to be left oily.

For the weekly cleaning, the gun should be stripped and the working parts dried and inspected before being re-oiled. When the barrel is cleaned, great care must be exercised to ensure that no damage is inflicted, whether the cleaning rod or the double pull through is used. It is not proposed to go through all the details of the examination and tests of the various parts, most of which will be apparent by the use of common-sense. There are, however, three parts of the gun which should be weighed, for which the following instructions may be found of help :—

FIRSTLY, THE FUSEE SPRING. This should weigh between 8 and 10 lbs. To ascertain and, if necessary, adjust, proceed as follows :—Take out the lock and place the loop of the spring balance over the knob of the crank handle. Rest the wrist on the casing and pull the balance slowly upwards ; the weight of the spring is that shown on the scale when the knob begins to move. If the weight is not correct, adjust by use of the vice spring at the front of the fusee box. To increase the weight turn the pin downwards and vice-versa.

Three turns are equal to about $\frac{1}{2}$ lb.

SECONDLY, THE LOCK SPRING. This should weigh between 12 and 14 lbs. To check this weight, remove the lock from the gun and place it on a level surface. Place the loop of the balance over the side lever head. The weight will be registered when the tumbler begins to rotate. If the lock spring has weakened, it will be necessary to replace it.

THIRDLY, THE WEIGHT OF THE RE-COILING PARTS. These should not weigh more than 4 lbs. To check this weight, remove the fusee spring and place the crank handle vertical.

Put the loop of the balance over the right end of the crankshaft and pull to the rear.

Excessive weight is probably due to lack of oil or excessive packing of the barrel.

Before firing, the gun must be thoroughly examined. All parts should be well oiled and the barrel, muzzle cup and muzzle attachment, then wiped dry.

Water supply and belt boxes must be properly inspected and the traversing handles filled with oil.

During firing, special attention must be given to ensure that the water supply is kept up. Oil should be freely used during all intervals. The tripod must be inspected to see that the jamming handles are properly tight.

After firing, the gun should be stripped as soon as possible, and every part cleaned and prepared for further action.

The belts must be cleaned and, if necessary, dried before being refilled.

The tripod should be oiled and overhauled.

STRIPPING AND ASSEMBLING

When stripping the gun, care must be exercised to ensure that the correct tools, when required, are employed and that force is avoided, paying particular attention to the following points :—

Before closing the front cover, be certain that the feedblock is properly in position and that the slide is to the left.

Before closing the rear cover, be certain that the lock is properly in the gun.

Beware of straining the hinges of both covers.

Before releasing the lock spring, be sure the

extractor is right up, to ensure that the firing pin hole is opposite the firing pin.

Before opening the rear cases, always pull the crank handle to the rear.

TO STRIP THE GUN, remove the recoiling parts in the following order :—

1. Lock. Unload, pull back the crank handle, open the rear cover and remove the lock, taking care to place the left thumb between the top edge of the extractor and the stop on the lock casing before removal.

2. Muzzle attachment. Take out the split pin and remove the outer casing. Unscrew and remove the cup.

3. Feedblock. Open the front cover and lift out.

4. Fusee spring box. Place the right hand behind and the left hand at the front of the box, push forward, and release it from the studs. Disconnect the fusee chain and remove the box and spring.

5. Fusee. Turn slightly to the rear and lift off the fusee and chain.

6. Barrel and side plates. Raise the rear cover and lower the crosspiece by taking out the T fixing pin on the left side. Take out the slide on each side and draw out the side plates and barrel.

To re-assemble, place the parts back in the opposite order, ensuring that each is correctly in position and that no force is used.

TO STRIP THE LOCK.

(N.B.—The handle of the T fixing pin is made for use in forcing out the various parts if they are tight.)

1. Cock the lock.
2. Take out side lever split pin and bush.
3. Remove side levers, extractor levers and extractor.
4. Take out tumbler axis pin and tumbler.
5. Release lock spring (by depressing tail of sear).
6. Take out trigger axis pin and trigger.
7. Take out lock spring, fixing pin and sear (with spring attached).

TO RE-ASSEMBLE.　Replace in the following order :—

1. Sear and spring.
2. Firing pin.
3. Tumbler and axis pin.
4. Trigger and axis pin.
5. Extractor, extractor levers and side levers.
6. Side lever split pin and bush.
7. Force home lock spring between trigger and extractor with long arm towards extractor.

N.B.—Before inserting spring see that lock is

in the fired position (to give spring as much room as possible), by drawing the tails of the trigger and tumbler to the rear.

STOPPAGE AND IMMEDIATE ACTION

The gun occasionally suffers from mechanical faults. These faults or stoppages come under two headings, prolonged or temporary.

Prolonged stoppages are due to the failure of some part for which spare parts are not carried, and which cannot be repaired without proper tools and preparation. Such stoppages naturally put the gun out of action for an indefinite period, and the assistance of the armourer should be called upon as soon as possible.

Temporary stoppages are those which can be rectified on the spot by normal immediate action. With proper care, such stoppages are largely avoidable, and, with a well trained team, they rarely occur. The main reasons for temporary stoppages are :—

LACK OF ATTENTION TO THE POINTS BEFORE FIRING, *e.g.*, failure to see that the gun is properly oiled, or failure to check the weights of the fusee spring or recoiling parts carefully.

LACK OF ATTENTION TO THE POINTS
DURING FIRING, *e.g.*, failure to ensure
that the belt box is kept in the correct
position, failure to oil up thoroughly during
intervals in firing, or failure to see that there
is ample water in the barrel casing after
prolonged firing.

FAILURE OF A PART FOR WHICH A
SPARE IS CARRIED.

FAULTY AMMUNITION.

Constant practice during training will enable
the members of the team to know instinctively
how to cure any temporary stoppage. Immediate recognition of the probable cause of the
stoppage, instinctive knowledge of the action
necessary and prompt handling of the gun,
should ensure that the gun is firing again in
the matter of a few seconds. It cannot be
impressed too often that the saving of the " odd
seconds " may make all the difference in the heat
of action.

Normally, stoppages occur in one of four
recognised positions which are marked by the
crank handle. As the gun is very frequently
fired in the dark, it is absolutely necessary to
recognise the positions by feel as well as by
sight. Gun crews must learn, therefore, to feel
the crank handle as well as look at it, and they

should be trained to perform the immediate action blindfold.

FIRST POSITION.

The crank handle steps slightly behind the perpendicular.

A stoppage in this position shows that (with the exception of the last cause, which is specially explained) the lock has not travelled far enough to the rear to allow the extractor to drop.

The causes of this stoppage are :—

1. Weak charge in the ammunition (unavoidable and not likely to recur).
2. Too much weight on the fusee spring (lack of attention to the points before firing).
3. Want of oil in the recoiling parts or excessive friction (lack of attention to the points before firing).
4. Excessive packing round the barrel (failure to weigh the recoiling parts).
5. Worn barrel, causing the gas to lose part of its driving power (this may result from prolonged firing, or may be due to lack of proper inspection before coming into action).
6. Weak or broken gib. spring (unavoidable). Although the crank handle stops in the first position, it does so on the way forward. The lock moves fully to the rear and the

extractor drops, but owing to the weakness or breakage of the gib. spring, the point of the round is not held in line with the chamber and hits against the rear end of the barrel block.

The immediate action is to pull the crank handle on to the roller, pull the belt to the left and release the handle. (This does by hand what the gun has failed to do automatically). If the stoppage recurs, repeat the immediate action and lighten the fusee by turning it three clicks in the anti-clockwise direction. Each click is a half-turn, and three clicks make a difference of about half a pound in weight. If the crank handle stops in the first position on the way forward when carrying out the immediate action, pull back the crank handle on to the roller, raise the rear cover, clear the face of the extractor, change the lock, relay and carry on.

SECOND POSITION.

The crank handle stops slightly in front of the perpendicular.

A stoppage in this position indicates that the lock has moved correctly to the rear, that the extractor has dropped, but that there is some obstruction preventing the round entering the chamber fully.

The causes of this stoppage are :—

1. A damaged cartridge (this should have been apparent when the belt was being prepared).

2. A separated case, which adheres to the next cartridge and comes away from the chamber when that round is withdrawn (unavoidable unless it is repeated, when see the immediate action called for).

3. A separated case which remains in the chamber (unavoidable except as in the note above).

The immediate action is to pull back the crank handle and at the same time to call out " Clearing Plug." On hearing this, No. 2 at once gets the plug ready for use in case it should be required. Having drawn back the crank handle, No. 1 raises the rear cover and lifts up the lock. He examines the face of the extractor by feel, and if he feels that there is a damaged round, or a good round with the front portion of a separated case attached, he tells No. 2 that he does not want the clearing plug, clears the face of the extractor, replaces the lock, reloads relays, and carries on firing.

If No. 1 finds a good round on the face of the extractor, he removes it, replaces the lock, and while keeping the crank handle to the rear, inserts the clearing plug and removes the separated case which has stuck in the barrel. He then reloads, relays, and carries on.

If separated cases occur frequently, the connecting rod is too short and therefore not forcing the face of the extractor sufficiently tightly against the barrel clock. In this event, the collar on the connecting rod must be undone by means of the combination tool, and a washer inserted. The connecting rod is then replaced and the gun reloaded and relaid.

THIRD POSITION.

The crank handle stops before it quite reaches the check lever.

The causes of this stoppage are :—

1. A slight fault in the feed. (This can normally be prevented by proper inspection of the belts before getting into action, though when the belts are getting old, these slight faults are apt to occur).

2. Friction in the lock. (Avoidable by proper attention to the points before and during firing).

3. A bad fault in feed. (This arises from the belt or the long brass strips being in bad condition—or from the belt box being out of line with the feedlock. All these causes should be noticed and rectified in the points before or during firing).

4. Thick-rimmed cartridge (unavoidable).

When a stoppage occurs in the third position, No. 1 assumes at once that it is caused by a slight fault in the feed. The immediate action is to draw back the crank handle slightly, pull the belt to the left, release the crank handle, and then strike it down on to the check lever ; relay and carry on. If the gun fires a few rounds and then stops again, No. 1 repeats the immediate action, but after striking the extractor on to the check lever, he unloads, oils up and reloads, relays and carries on firing.

If when No. 1 tries to perform the immediate action he finds that he cannot do so, he feels the slide of the feedblock ; this will either be loose or stuck fast. If it is jammed, No. 1 calls out "Feedblock," and forces the crank handle back on to the roller, though in order to do so he may have to call on No. 2 to assist by forcing down the horns of the extractor, which he does with any tool at hand, after opening the front cover. No. 1 now raises the rear cover and lays the lock on the top of the casing. No. 1 now draws the recoiling parts to the rear, while No. 2 removes the belt. No. 1 now allows the recoiling parts to move forward again, and No. 2 straightens the round in the belt and inspects the belt itself. No. 1 then replaces the lock in the gun, and keeping the crank handle to the rear, closes the rear cover, pulls the belt to the left, releases the crank handle, relays and carries on.

If the slide is free, No. 1 calls out " Extractor " and opens the front cover. No. 2 forces down the extractor, and No. 1 then withdraws the lock to the rear, takes it out, and clears the face of the extractor. Meantime No. 2 has withdrawn the belt from the feedblock and removed the first round (which is the one which has caused the trouble) from the belt.

No. 1 then replaces the lock, fastens the front cover, reloads, relays and carries on.

FOURTH POSITION.

The crank handle stops right home on the check lever. A stoppage in this position means that there has been no explosion, or such a weak one that the lock has not been forced to the rear.

The cause of stoppages in the fourth position is :—

1. Misfire (unavoidable).
2. Broken firing pin (unavoidable).
3. Broken lock spring (unavoidable).
4. Empty pocket in the belt (avoidable by proper attention to the points before firing) The immediate action is to pull the crank

handle on to the roller, pull the belt to the left, release the crank handle, relay and carry on.

If the gun still does not fire, then unload, change the lock, reload, relay and carry on.

If, when performing the original immediate action, No. 1 finds that the belt comes through the feedblock more than expected, he repeats the immediate action, *i.e.*, goes through the second half of the loading action, relays and carries on.

There are a few unusual stoppages which are very unlikely to occur, and which should not be studied until the team are thoroughly proficient in dealing with the normal stoppages dealt with above.

The principal unusual stoppages are :—

1. WHEN THE CRANK HANDLE STOPS RIGHT BACK ON THE ROLLER. The cause is a broken fusee spring (unavoidable), and the immediate action is to remove the fusee spring and box, pull the belt to the left, turn the crank handle on to the check lever, replace the new spring, weigh the spring, relay and carry on.

2. WHEN THE GUN STOPS IN NO. 4 POSITION, and after the normal immediate action, fires two rounds and stops again.

The cause is a damaged feedblock (unavoidable), and the immediate action is to take the spare feedblock into service.

3. WHEN THE GUN DOES NOT STOP FIRING, although the thumbpiece is released. No. 1 removes a round from the belt, and the gun must stop when the empty pocket is in the feedblock. When the gun has stopped, No. 1 pulls the crank handle on to the roller, and No. 2 removes the belt. No. 1 then releases the crank handle, goes through the unloading motions, and changes the lock.

PERSONNEL

The gun team consists of an N.C.O., who is responsible for discipline and fire control, and six men, numbered from 1 to 6.

No. 1 fires the gun in action and looks after it at other times. During the bringing of the gun into action, he takes charge of the tripod and mounts it under the direction of the N.C.O. He is responsible for ensuring that everything about the gun is in good order, that the tripod is correctly mounted, and that the fire orders are properly understood and carried out.

No. 2 brings the gun into action and sees that

the sliding dust cover on the bottom of the breech casing is opened. During firing he sees that the proper supply of S.A.A. is maintained and that the belt boxes are in position. He assists and understudies No. 1.

No. 3 is responsible for keeping No. 2 supplied with full belts, and for the spare part box.

Nos. 4, 5 and 6 are employed in filling used belts, and are at the same time ready to replace casualties to Nos. 1, 2 or 3.

LOADING, FIRING AND UNLOADING

When the gun is mounted on the tripod, No. 1 should be seated behind the gun in the proper firing position. He must be in a comfortable position, with his elbows resting on the insides of his thighs. He must hold the gun correctly. Thumbs should be on the thumbpiece. First fingers should be over the top of the rear crosspiece, pressing slightly on the gun and keeping it steady when firing. Middle fingers should be behind the safety catch, and the remaining fingers round the barrel handles (which are also oil bottles).

No. 2 lies on the right of the gun, in a position enabling him to see No. 1 and also the N.C.O. in charge. He must ensure that the belt is the right way round and the box in line with the feedlock opening. If the box is not straight a stoppage is almost inevitable.

On the command " Load," No. 2 undoes the belt box, takes the tab of the belt in his left hand, and passes it through the feedlock from right to left.

No. 1, on hearing the command " Load," pulls the crank handle to the rear. (This draws back the lock and extractor, and the latter drops on reaching the rear position).

He then takes the tab of the belt which No. 2 has passed through the feedlock, and pulls it sharply to the left. (This action places the first round in the belt into position, where it will be gripped by the extractor).

He then releases the crank handle, which flies forward under the influence of the fusee spring. In releasing the crank handle, care must be taken that the forward movement is not checked. (When the lock is home, the extractor rises and grips the round in the feedlock).

The gun is now half loaded.

No. 1 then repeats the movements. He draws back the crank handle. (This withdraws the first round in the belt on the face of the extractor, which drops at the rear and places the round in line with the chamber). Then he pulls the belt to the left again. (This places the second round of the belt in position). Then he releases the crank handle. (This time, as the lock goes forward, the first round is placed in the chamber, and when the extractor rises, the second round is gripped).

The gun is now fully loaded.

In loading No. 1 must make certain that the movements are not slurred. Each must be complete before the next is begun, if faults in loading are to be avoided. When the correct range has been placed on the target slide, and a target correctly recognised, direction and elevation are obtained with the elevating wheel on the tripod, and by striking the rear crosspiece with whichever hand is necessary. No. 1 should always maintain his hold of the gun with the hand that is not used for traversing.

On the command "Fire," No. 1 raises the safety catch with his middle fingers and pushes in the thumbpiece with his thumbs. This draws back the trigger bar which runs along the inside of the rear cover, releases the trigger from the mechanism inside the lock, and allows the firing pin to fly forward and fire the gun.

The recoil and gases send the recoiling parts to the rear, the fusee spring takes them forward again, and the gun continues to fire while pressure is maintained on the thumbpiece.

Fire is normally maintained in bursts of about 25 rounds, or about 3 seconds, and the aim is checked at intervals. During firing, however, No. 1 should not gaze fixedly along the sights; he should try and observe the result of his fire by direct observation, only using the sights when desirous of checking his aim.

On the command " Cease Fire," pressure on the thumbpiece is released. The thumbpiece is replaced by a spring, the safety catch automatically falls into position, the trigger is allowed to engage in the mechanism in the lock, and the gun stops. There will be a live round in the chamber and another gripped in the feedblock.

On the command " Unload," No. 1 pulls back the crank handle to the rear (this withdraws the live round from the chamber for ejection and the round from the feedblock; when the lock reaches the rear the extractor falls, and places the round from the feedblock in line with the chamber). He then releases the crank handle, which flies forward. (This places the round in the chamber, but as the belt was not pulled to the left, the extractor, when it rises, does not grip another round).

No. 1 then repeats the action. First he pulls back the crank handle. (This withdraws the round just placed in the chamber and ejects it. No round is drawn from the feedblock). Then he releases the crank handle. (There is no round this time to go into the chamber, and no round in the feedblock to be gripped).

No. 1 then raises the safety catch and eases the spring by pushing in the thumbpiece, replaces the slide of the tangent sight at zero, and the gun is unloaded.

No. 2 immediately replaces the partly used belt with a new one, and sends back the one withdrawn to the rear for re-filling.

Nos. 1 and 2 then oil up and go through the points during firing.

TARGETS

Owing to the shape of the cone produced by bursts of Machine Gun fire, the Machine Gun is particularly adapted to engage targets which are narrow but deep, and is therefore essentially a weapon for enfilade fire. Whenever possible the guns should be situated so that their fields of fire cross diagonally. To engage targets directly on front of the position is wasteful, and allows the enemy the possibility of passing between the cones of fire.

By the use of traversing, relatively wide targets can, nevertheless, be engaged, while the combined use of the elevating wheel and traversing makes diagonal targets also vulnerable.

The study of overhead and indirect fire is rather too deep for explanation in this manual, though both are of great value, particularly in static warfare.

THOMPSON SUB-MACHINE GUN

The Sub-Machine Gun is particularly adapted to close-quarter fighting, and to fighting in circumstances where targets may be expected to appear without warning at relatively short ranges. The gun can be fired from the shoulder, or by the sense of direction, from the waist. Targets can be engaged with great rapidity, and changes of front can be made much more quickly than with the rifle.

The gun fires a .45 bullet which is fed from two types of magazine, which are explained later.

The gun weighs about 10 lbs., and is very comfortable to handle.

It can be set to fire single shots or in bursts. A good gunner can produce about 40 well aimed shots in a minute, while bursts of fire, which are not generally used, should not exceed 3 to 4 rounds, and are fired at the rate of nearly 1,000 rounds per minute.

MAGAZINE FILLING

The ammunition is carried in two distinct forms of magazine :—

1. THE BOX TYPE MAGAZINE. This is like an elongated rifle magazine, and consists of a box, platform and spring. It holds 20 rounds, which are placed in position separately by being pressed down and back. The magazine is held during filling in the left hand, with the ribs away from the body.

2. THE DRUM TYPE MAGAZINE. This type holds 50 rounds. To load the drum :—

(a) Raise the flat spring of the winding key on the cover of the drum, and slide off the key.

(b) Lift off the cover.

(c) Turn the rotor which is thus disclosed in the drum in a clockwise direction, until any one of the claws is opposite the mouth of the drum.

(d) Commencing from the outside, place five rounds in each compartment, beginning with the one opposite the mouth and working anti-clockwise. The bullets point upwards. The shape of the fittings in the drum causes the filling to work spirally towards the centre until the drum is full.

(e) Replace the cover, ensuring that the small recess in the cover fits over the stud fixed on the drum.

(f) Replace the winding key by seeing that it slides over the flat sides of the centre stud.

(*g*) Turn the winding key the requisite number of clicks in a clockwise direction—the number being determined as follows :—

1. If the gun was manufactured in or before 1921, 11 clicks.

2. If after 1921, 9 clicks, the later models being slightly smaller.

These instructions are set out on a plate on the cover of the drum. The date of manufacture is on the bottom of the drum.

(*Every member of the team should know the date of manufacture of each drum, as they may have to be filled in the dark*).

LOADING

1. To load with the box type magazine, hold the gun comfortably with the right hand, the butt resting on the hip and the muzzle pointing well up.

Pull the crank handle back with the left hand to its full extent.

With the left hand place the magazine in position, with its ribs engaging in the corresponding recess in the trigger guard, and force upwards. It is often necessary when the gun is new to raise the magazine catch to allow the magazine to rise sufficiently to become engaged, but after use the magazine moves into position without difficulty.

Place the safety catch to Safety by turning to the rear.

N.B.—The safety catch can only be applied when the gun is cocked. The change lever can only be moved from automatic to single shots when the gun is cocked. (The change lever can be moved from single shots to automatic at any time).

2. To load with the drum type magazine, hold the gun and cock it as with the box type. Hold the drum in the left hand, with the winding key to the front. Engage the two ribs near the mouth of the drum in the horizontal grooves in the front of the body, and slide the drum from left to right. The drum will engage when central. Place the safety catch to Safe.

UNLOADING

1. To unload with the box magazine, press the magazine catch on the left side of the pistol grip with the left thumb. Hold the magazine with the fingers of the left hand and pull it down. Put the safety catch forward. Allow the action to move forward under control by pressing the trigger while holding the cocking handle with the left hand. Cock the gun and

inspect the chamber. Then allow the action to move forward again under control as before.

N.B.—Owing to the risk of damage, the action is never allowed to go forward except under control, as explained above.

2. To unload with the drum magazine, cock the gun; press the magazine catch up with the left thumb and grip the magazine with the fingers of the left hand—index finger on one side, and the other fingers on the other side. Slide the magazine out to the left. Then allow the action to go forward and proceed as with the box magazine.

N.B.—When the magazine is empty the working parts stop in the forward position when the drum type magazine is in use—in contrast to when the box type is used, and the gun stops with the working parts to the rear.

HOLDING THE GUN FOR ACTION

The gun can be fired from the waist or the shoulder. For both the position of the legs and the body is the same. The left leg is advanced and pointed to the target. The left knee is bent and the weight of the body thrown forward. The right leg is kept braced.

To fire from the waist the butt is gripped between the body and the right elbow. The right hand grasps the pistol grip, and the left hand the fore-grip. THE GUN IS ALWAYS AIMED LOW, AS IT THROWS HIGH.

To fire from the shoulder, the right elbow should be well raised and the gun pulled well back to the shoulder.

There is no recoil when the gun fires.

AIMING

There is an aperture backsight with a leaf graduated up to 600 yards. For very short ranges, *i.e.*, about 50 yards, sighting can be obtained by using the cutaway portion of the crank handle as a backsight.

Generally the gun is fired from the waist by sense of direction, and no sights are used.

FIRING

Single shots are generally used. The speed with which these can be fired makes bursts unnecessarily wasteful. When employed, bursts should be kept as short as possible, and should not be used except in cases of emergency.

STOPPAGES AND IMMEDIATE ACTION

There is little call for immediate action, as the gun has no recognised stoppages except empty magazines.

When the drum magazine is empty it makes a rattling noise.

If the gun stops, change magazine, reload and carry on.

If the gun still fails to fire, recock, turn the gun over to the right, and try and shake out the round or empty case from the chamber. If it will not come, remove the magazine, when it will drop out. Then replace the magazine, reload and carry on.

N.B.—In practice the following stoppages have occurred :—

1. When the box magazine is in use, the gun sometimes stops because the spring in the magazine gets caught and does not force up the following round.

   The immediate action is to cock the gun, strike the magazine sharply upwards and carry on.

2. When the drum magazine is in use, two rounds are apt to try to enter the chamber simultaneously, particularly when the magazine is new and the spring inclined to be fierce.

   The immediate action is as laid down, *viz.*, recock, turn the gun over to the right and shake the rounds out, reload and carry on

MECHANISM

The gun is operated by the direct effect of the gases generated by the firing of the rounds and a recoil spring.

The gases, while forcing the bullet through the barrel simultaneously (except for a slight check occasioned by a spring in the front of the bolt), force the bolt to the rear. When the gases reach the front of the barrel, they pass upwards through the vents of the compensator and tend to depress the gun, and so counteract its tendency to throw high. The recoil compresses the spring, which in turn takes the working parts forward again.

The trigger mechanism, extraction and ejection, are in principle similar to the rifle and light automatic rifle.

The safety catch is on the left side of the pistol grip, and can only be operated when the gun is cocked.

The change lever is just in front of the safety catch, and is placed upright for single shots and forward for bursts.

CARE OF THE GUN

To clean the barrel, cock the gun and put the safety catch to Safe. Care must be exercised when using the cleaning rod, to secure that damage to the bolt face is avoided.

Before firing, the barrel must be wiped dry, but the chamber must be left oiled, together with all working parts and the pads on either side of the boltway. After oiling is completed, place the change lever at Automatic and work the cocking handle several times to ensure distribution of oil.

Oil up as frequently as possible during firing.

After firing is finished, all parts must be left thoroughly oiled.

ANTI-TANK RIFLE

The Anti-Tank Rifle is a single shot hand-operated weapon. It is designed to afford the means of stopping light enemy armoured tanks, but is not constructed to engage the heaviest types.

Best results are obtained when aim is taken at the crew of the tank, rather than at the machine itself. Accuracy of aim is therefore of very great importance.

The rifle weighs 36 lbs., and is little under 5 ft. 6 in. in length. The magazine, loaded with 5 rounds, weighs nearly $2\frac{1}{2}$ lbs. The cartridge has a calibre of .55 in.

DESCRIPTION

The rifle is fitted with a bipod front support. To open this support, the retaining catch is depressed and the support swung away from the barrel. The catch will engage automatically when the support is fully open. When opened, the legs can be extended telescopically to permit of firing over obstacles.

The firer lies directly behind the rifle. He holds it firmly into his shoulder with his left hand by means of a spade grip at the butt end, and grasps the pistol grip with his right hand. The right cheek must be pressed against the rifle, *well forward on the cheek rest and clear of the spade grip and shoulder piece* to prevent bruising from the recoil. The force of the recoil is considerable, though much reduced by the recoil reducer and the padding fitted in the shoulder piece. The recoil reducer is an attachment at the forward end of the barrel, by means of which some of the gases following the bullet escape through vents and are directed to the rear of a disc which forms part of the recoil reducer. The gases, by striking this disc, tend to force the rifle forward and so operate against the force of the recoil.

MECHANISM

The mechanism is constructed on similar lines to that of the Service Rifle with which the Home Guard are acquainted, and it will not therefore be detailed here.

CARE OF THE RIFLE

The cleaning and general rules for care of the rifle are similar to those of the Service Rifle.

The recoil reducer must be thoroughly dry before firing to avoid the danger of oil smoke and fouling. After firing it should be cleaned and re-oiled.

On every occasion on which the recoil reducer is stripped, great care must be taken to ensure that it is replaced in exactly the same position to ensure correct re-assembly.

MAGAZINE FILLING

The magazine is also similar in construction to that of the Service Rifle. It is filled by each round being pressed separately on to the magazine platform.

LOADING

Turn the safety catch to the front. Place the magazine in the opening in the top of the body, inserting the front end first. Open and close the breech as with a Service Rifle. Bring the safety catch to the rear to apply.

CHANGING MAGAZINES

The bolt will not go forward when the magazine is empty, as the forward end of the bolt strikes the top of the magazine platform. Pull back the bolt to its full extent, press the magazine catch (which is situated immediately behind the magazine) forward with the palm of the right hand; hold and remove the magazine.

(After practice this should all be done in a continuous movement). Then replace with a full magazine, close the breech, and apply the safety catch.

UNLOADING

Turn the safety catch to the front and remove the magazine. Open and close the breech. Release the trigger and apply the safety catch.

SIGHTING

The rifle is fitted with a backsight set to two ranges only. The lever attached to the backsight raises the aperture to the elevation necessary. When the lever is turned to the left, the backsight is set for 300 yards. When turned to the right it is set for 500 yards.

At the longer range the bullet will pierce half-inch armour plate. The carrying range of the rifle is very long, certainly about double that of the Service Rifle, though naturally at longer ranges it is less capable of piercing armour plate.

AIMING

Aim is taken as with the Service Rifle. The point of aim should be one length ahead of a tank passing directly across the front, half a length in front of one advancing or retiring diagonally; and, of course, straight at one advancing or retiring directly in front of the rifle.

When, as is usual, the rifle is fired from a trench, traversing can be easily obtained by swinging the rifle in the direction desired, but this is not so easily done when lying in the open. Men must therefore be practised to obtain the required change of direction by moving round with the elbows remaining on the ground.

FIRING

The trigger has two pressures, and the rifle is fired as is the Service Rifle. The bolt is worked in the shoulder in exactly the same way. The rifle is naturally reloaded after the order "cease fire" has been given, and the safety catch then applied.

BROWNING AUTOMATIC RIFLE

The Browning Automatic Rifle is operated by recoil actuated by gas and a return spring. It is essentially a single shot weapon, but is so constructed that in case of emergency bursts of fire can be produced by automatic action at a very high rate.

The rifle weighs about 16 lbs.

The magazine, fully charged with 20 rounds, weighs 1¾ lbs.

The rifle fires .300 ammunition.

When the rifle is set for single shots, a good gunner can fire about 40 well-aimed shots in a minute.

When it is set for automatic firing, rounds are fired at approximately 900 rounds per minute.

Although the rifle is very accurate for single shot firing, it is very difficult to control when firing bursts.

DESCRIPTION

The barrel carries a flash eliminator, as the flash when firing bursts is particularly noticeable owing to the high rate achieved.

In the bottom of the barrel is the gas vent, giving access to the gas chamber and cylinder. The volume of gas which can pass into the chamber is regulated by varying-sized holes in the front end of the cylinder. Usually the smallest hole is employed, and the larger ones only taken into use should the rifle fire sluggishly or should faults in extraction or ejection recur. Such faults are usually avoidable by proper attention to the care of the rifle. In the gas cylinder is the piston which is driven to the rear by the gas, and in its rear end by lugs fitted in grooves in the body.

The gas cylinder is covered by the forehand grip, which is kept in position by a retaining pin.

Behind the cylinder and return spring is the trigger group.

The change lever is on the left side of the trigger guard, and can be set in three positions, *viz*. :—

Forward (marked " F ") for firing single shots.

Upright (marked " A ") for firing in bursts.

Back (marked " S ") for safety.

In order to place the lever at " S " a small knob on the left of the body must be pushed in.

The trigger mechanism is similar to that of the ordinary rifle, except when the lever is at " A." In this event the sear is kept depressed as long as pressure is maintained on the trigger, and the bolt is allowed to continue to travel backwards and forwards without interference.

When the lever is at " S " the sear is disengaged from the trigger, and therefore cannot be released from the bend of the piston.

The rear end of the piston carries the hammer, and is attached to the bolt by a link and pin.

When each round is fully home, the hammer is forced against the rear end of the firing pin, which goes forward on to the cap and fires the charge.

The gas then drives the working parts again to the rear.

The rifle always stops with the recoiling parts to the rear, excepting in the case of an empty magazine. It invariably stops with an empty chamber.

MECHANISM

When the rifle is fired, some of the gases following the bullet through the barrel pass through the gas vent into the gas cylinder. They force the piston to the rear and thus compress the return spring. The piston carries the bolt with it, and the empty case being gripped by the extractor is carried towards the rear until it comes in contact with the ejector on the left side of the boltway and is ejected to the right.

When the piston is stopped in its backward movement by the buffer, the return spring takes command and forces it forward, carrying the bolt and firing mechanism with it.

In its passage forward, the lug on the lower part of the bolt strikes the base of the top round in the magazine and carries it up into the chamber. The base of the cartridge slides up the face of the bolt and is engaged behind the extractor.

When the bolt is fully home the hammer strikes against the rear of the firing pin, which is forced forward on to the base of the cartridge and fires the charge.

STOPPAGES AND IMMEDIATE ACTION

The rifle in the ordinary way does not stop, excepting when the magazine is empty. Very occasionally cases of faulty extraction or ejection occur, but they are usually attributable to lack of attention before coming into action.

The immediate action, therefore, is always that for an empty magazine, *viz.*, remove the magazine, replace a full one, recock, relay and carry on.

In the event of the rifle still failing to fire, remove the magazine and look for an obstruction in the chamber or body. Remove this, replace the magazine, recock, relay and carry on. If faulty extraction or ejection persists, increase the supply of gas to the cylinder by turning the next larger hole in the gas chamber opposite the hole in the barrel.

At the first opportunity the rifle should be thoroughly cleaned, particular attention being paid to those parts which may be affected by the gas, and the gas regulator reset at the smallest hole.

MAGAZINE FILLING

The magazine is similar in construction to that of the Service Rifle. It is filled in the same way. The full load is 20 rounds, but when ammunition is to be left in the magazine for a considerable time, not more than 15 rounds should be put in, to prevent possible deterioration of the spring.

LOADING

The rifle is not loaded in the same way as the Service Rifle or Machine Gun. At no time is a round in the chamber ready for the trigger to be pressed.

In this rifle the magazine must be placed in the aperture in the body, and forced home when it will be retained in position by a spring. The cocking handle is then drawn to the rear and pushed forward again. The safety catch is put to safety. The rifle is then ready to come into action.

N.B.—When the cocking handle is drawn to the rear, it brings the working parts with it and cocks the gun. When it is pushed forward, it moves independently and leaves the working parts to the rear. The cocking handle does not move backwards and forwards during either single shot firing or firing by bursts.

SIGHTING

The battle sight should always be used up to 400 yards.

The backsight is of the aperture pattern. It is graduated in 100 yards up to 900 yards, and then in 50 yards up to 1,600 yards.

The slide is operated by a press catch on the right of the leaf, and is marked with a line which should be opposite the range required.

FIRING

The rifle has a single pressure.

The normal method of fire is by single shots. The trigger must be fully released after each shot, because until it is so released it remains disengaged from the sear, and renewed pressure on it will not fire the rifle. To ensure correct release, the trigger finger should be taken right off the trigger momentarily. If firing is by bursts, they should be kept down to as short bursts as possible. The rifle must be re-aimed after each burst, as it is very difficult to maintain aim—the gun almost invariably jumping to the right.

UNLOADING

See that the change lever is at " A " or " F."
Push the magazine catch in the front of the trigger guard and remove the magazine.
Press the trigger.
Cock the rifle and inspect the chamber.
Press the trigger again.
The gun is then properly unloaded.

CARE OF THE RIFLE

When not in use the rifle will be kept well oiled. It is a feature of American guns and rifles that they require more oil than those of British pattern.

When cleaning the barrel, the rifle is cocked and the change lever placed at safety. When the cleaning rod is used, care must be exercised to ensure that damage to the face of the bolt is avoided.

When preparing the rifle for firing, the barrel should be wiped dry, all other parts being left thoroughly oiled. The gas regulator must be inspected to ensure that the correct hole is in position and that the vents are clean and unobstructed.

During intervals of firing all recoiling parts should be re-oiled and the gas vents inspected.

After firing, the usual thorough cleaning is necessary. All magazines should be inspected, cleaned and refilled at the first opportunity.

THE LEWIS GUN

BY A SPECIAL CONTRIBUTOR

This weapon is a light .303 automatic gun —gas operated—air cooled—magazine fed.

The gun presents a small target, and in action is operated by a team of two. The firer behind the gun—known as No. 1, and with him, lying beside the gun, is No. 2, whose job it is to change the magazines when needed, and who in actual fact acts as " fuel feeder."

The gun fires at the rate of 10 rounds per second, and a trained man can fire with accuracy up to 150 rounds per minute.

The gun in action weighs 26-28 lbs.

The magazine, when full, weighs $4\frac{1}{8}$ lbs., when empty $1\frac{1}{2}$ lbs., and holds 47 rounds.

DESCRIPTION

The overall length of the gun is $50\frac{1}{2}$ inches, the barrel being $26\frac{1}{4}$ inches long.

The gun, as stated before, is air cooled. To bring this about a radiator casing is built round the actual barrel itself. Inside are the radiator flanges (much the same as a fishes gills). The radiator casing is built out a few inches beyond the mouth of the barrel, causing suction on firing and thus drawing the cool air round the flanges from the rear end of the radiator casing.

In the bottom of the barrel is found the gas vent, through which passes the gas after a round has been fired; the gas, in its turn, forces the piston back.

Just in front of the trigger guard is found the return spring contained in the pinion. By a rack on the underneath of the pinion, the spring is wound up, thus driving the piston forward on the next action. The piston is made in one piece with the striker. Therefore, as the piston comes forward, with it comes the striker, and the round is then fired.

The whole action then repeats itself until finger pressure is taken off the trigger.

The gun is made up of three main groups :—

(a) The barrel group, consisting of the barrel itself, the outer casing surrounding it, and the gas vent and key.

(b) The piston group, consisting of the piston and bolt incorporating the striker. Working in conjunction with the piston is the pinion group.

(c) The butt group, consisting of the butt itself, inside which is found the oil bottle and drum.

Covering the bolt and inside working parts of the gun is the body cover—a metal plate placed in the rear of the magazine. The body cover can only be removed when the magazine is off.

On the right of the gun is the cocking handle. When the cocking handle is right forward, the gun is safe. When it is drawn right back, the gun is loaded. Remember never to keep the cocking handle in the backward position more than can be helped, as this weakens the return spring.

The magazine consists of a round pan (like a large biscuit), with a rotatable centre block.

In order to load, a loading handle is required. This is placed through the recess of the centre block, and is turned by hand to allow each round to fall in position.

LOADING

Place a filled magazine on magazine plate or post, making certain that the cocking handle is in the forward position.

Gently rotate magazine backwards and forwards until it slips over post and catch engages (keep the white disc on magazine to rear). Then with right hand rotate magazine until it will move no further.

Then pull back the cocking handle and gun is ready for firing.

NOTE.—To unload without firing, pull back your cocking handle and remove the magazine. Depress the base of your live round under the cartridge guide, with a point of a bullet. Then draw round forward until it points over feed arm, below body cover.

Always hold the cocking handle back with your right hand, then press trigger with your left, allowing the cocking handle to come slowly half-way forward. The bolt will then automatically press against the round, and push it clear of the cartridge guide. Pull back cocking handle to rear position, release the pressure on the trigger, and the round will then come out quite easily.

From the initial description of the gun, it will be seen that on release of the trigger the cocking handle will always be left in the rear position, ready for immediate firing on the trigger being pressed again.

Should the gun cease firing with the handle in the forward position, most probably the magazine is empty. An empty magazine will rotate freely on the gun.

There are two main actions involved in the firing of the gun, *i.e.* :—

1.—THE BACKWARD ACTION.—The piston

is driven back by the gases formed by the firing of the round. This, as previously explained, winds up the return spring.

2.—THE FORWARD ACTION.—The piston is driven forward, taking with it the striker and thus firing the round.

The firing of the gun relies, naturally, on the proper functioning of the return spring. If the tension is not enough to drive the piston forward, the gun will obviously *not* fire. This tension can quite easily be increased or decreased as required.

To increase the return spring, first remove butt by pushing in catch, and turning butt in anti-clockwise position. Then ease piston back, holding pinion group with left hand. Then with right hand draw the piston back, thus deducting return spring to required weight. Allow pinion to drop, push cocking handle to forward position, and re-assemble gun.

For decreasing weight, leaving locking handle back, hold pinion group in position, and slide piston forward.

The normal weight for return spring should be 12/14 lbs.

For measuring weight, a spring balance is supplied.

For the purposes of Home Guard training,

more intricate mechanical details are apt to be muddling. These can and should be picked up in a very short while in actual practice.

CARE OF GUN

This is the same as for any other weapon. *Never* put too much *oil* on the parts.

Keep the gas cylinder, and any parts that come in contact with gas, *completely free of oil.*

Inspect your gun daily, when possible, and certainly two or three times per week.

Before firing, see that all gas parts are dry, and remove oil from barrel. Weigh your return spring, and make certain that all parts of the gun are quite firm.

Examine your ammunition, and see that the magazines are correctly filled. Immediately after firing, unload, and clear your gun. Then strip down gun, clean thoroughly and oil. If possible, pour boiling water down the barrel.

Re-examine all magazines, and carry out any repairs.

During firing, by this is meant, a temporary cessation of fire. Slightly alter, if necessary, and adjust your mounting. Oil your magazine post, should it be needed, weigh your return spring, and place a full magazine on the gun and reload. If possible, send back empty magazines and send for filled ones.

STOPPAGES

The Lewis Gun, as any other automatic weapon, is liable to stoppages.

The aim of any man in charge of a gun, who has a stoppage, is to get his gun firing *as soon as possible again*.

Stoppages can either be temporary or prolonged. Temporary stoppages can be cured by immediate action. Very often it will be found that these are due to neglect, either before or after firing. Prolonged stoppages will involve stripping the gun to remedy it.

Immediate action can be applied to most stoppages, the others can be rectified by having a thorough working knowledge of the parts of the gun.

Whenever a stoppage occurs, feel *first* for the position of your cocking handle.

The following list of stoppages are the most likely to occur :—

Cocking handle stops in forward position—

1. Empty magazine.
2. Misfire—defective round.
3. Damaged or worn magazine.
4. Broken or faulty striker.

Cocking handle stops in backward position—

1. Faulty round (hard extraction).
   Faulty round (separated case).

2. Excessive friction or fouling (oil).
3. Fault in feed.
4. Broken or dirty extractor.
5. Broken piece of metal in boltway.

If the cocking handle stops in any other position, you have a broken spring, and must renew it before you can fire the gun again.

There are other stoppages that may occur, but they are not so common, and a good working knowledge of the gun is essential before attempting to rectify them.

TARGETS

Enfilade fire, as in any other weapon, can be used very effectively with a Lewis. Small groups of troops are an ideal target, and the use of the Lewis Gun against aircraft is most effective. The volume of fire can naturally be greatly increased by working with pairs of guns. This also means that should a stoppage occur in one gun, the other can still remain in action.

An effective and accurate range is 600-800 yards.

Finally, team work is absolutely essential. As in the case of the Vickers M.G., the will to do a little better than the next man will automatically lead to a very high standard of efficiency.

www.ingramcontent.com/pod-product-compliance
Lightning Source LLC
LaVergne TN
LVHW051803080426
835511LV00018B/3392